Sense of Touch

Carey Molter

Published by SandCastle™, an imprint of ABDO Publishing Company, 4940 Viking Drive, Edina, Minnesota 55435.

Printed in the United States.

Photo credits: Comstock, Corbis Images, Eyewire Images, Image 100, PhotoDisc, Rubberball

Library of Congress Cataloging-in-Publication Data

Molter, Carey, 1973-
  Sense of touch / Carey Molter.
     p. cm. -- (The senses)
  Includes index.
  ISBN 1-57765-630-X
     1. Touch--Juvenile literature. [1. Touch. 2. Senses and sensation.] I. Title.

QP451 .M68 2001
612.8'8--dc21

2001022902

The SandCastle concept, content, and reading method have been reviewed and approved by a national advisory board including literacy specialists, librarians, elementary school teachers, early childhood education professionals, and parents.

Let Us Know

After reading the book, SandCastle would like you to tell us your stories about reading. What is your favorite page? Was there something hard that you needed help with? Share the ups and downs of learning to read. We want to hear from you! To get posted on the Abdo Publishing Company Web site, send us email at:

sandcastle@abdopub.com

About SandCastle™

Nonfiction books for the beginning reader

- Basic concepts of phonics are incorporated with integrated language methods of reading instruction. Most words are short, and phrases, letter sounds, and word sounds are repeated.

- Readability is determined by the number of words in each sentence, the number of characters in each word, and word lists based on curriculum frameworks.

- Full-color photography reinforces word meanings and concepts.

- "Words I Can Read" list at the end of each book teaches basic elements of grammar, helps the reader recognize the words in the text, and builds vocabulary.

- Reading levels are indicated by the number of flags on the castle.

Look for more SandCastle books in these three reading levels:

Level 1 (one flag)	**Level 2** (two flags)	**Level 3** (three flags)
SandCastle 1	SandCastle 2	SandCastle 3
Grades Pre-K to K 5 or fewer words per page	**Grades K to 1** 5 to 10 words per page	**Grades 1 to 2** 10 to 15 words per page

Our senses tell us what
is happening around us.

Touch is one of our five senses.

Touch is how we know
what things feel like.

Clark feels the bumpy
shells in the rough sand.

Clara hugs the furry bunny.

It feels soft and warm.

Things that are wet often
feel cool and smooth.

Amy slips across the wet slide.

The puppy licks Kate.

It feels funny.

What do you think this
ground feels like?

Words I Can Read

Nouns

A **noun** is a person, place, or thing

bunny (BUHN-ee) p. 13

ground (GROUND) p. 21

puppy (PUHP-ee) p. 19

sand (SAND) p. 11

slide (SLIDE) p. 17

touch (TUHCH) pp. 7, 9

Plural Nouns

A **plural noun** is more than one person, place, or thing

senses (SENSS-ez) pp. 5, 7

shells (SHELZ) p. 11

things (THINGZ) pp. 9, 15

Proper Nouns

A **proper noun** is the name of a person, place, or thing

Amy (AYM-ee) p. 17

Clara (KLAIR-uh) p. 13

Clark (KLARK) p. 11

Kate (KAYT) p. 19

Verbs

A verb is an action or being word

are (AR) p. 15
do (DOO) p. 21
is (IZ) pp. 5, 7, 9
feel (FEEL) pp. 9, 15
feels (FEELZ)
  pp. 11, 13, 19, 21
happening
  (HAP-uhn-ing) p. 5

hugs (HUHGZ) p. 13
know (NOH) p. 9
licks (LIKSS) p. 19
slips (SLIPSS) p. 17
tell (TEL) p. 5
think (THINGK) p. 21

Adjectives

An adjective describes something

bumpy (BUHMP-ee) p. 11
cool (KOOL) p. 15
five (FIVE) p. 7
funny (FUHN-ee) p. 19
furry (FUR-ee) p. 13
one (WUHN) p. 7

rough (RUHF) p. 11
smooth (SMOOTH) p. 15
soft (SAWFT) p. 13
this (THISS) p. 21
warm (WORM) p. 13
wet (WET) pp. 15, 17

23

More About the Sense of Touch
Match the Words to their Pictures

sharp

dry

sticky

hot